# Fishes
# Of Lake Nipissing

Carsten R. Jorgensen

CARSTEN R. JORGENSEN

Copyright © 2018 Carsten R. Jorgensen

All rights reserved.

Written and published in Canada.

ISBN: 0994933843
ISBN-13: 978-0-9949338-4-3

# CONTENTS

# ACKNOWLEDGMENTS

All images in this book are known or thought to be public domain.

Cover design by Dana Woodard

Image on back cover is compliments of Lorri Lang who has graciously provided the photo on the pixabay.com website as a public domain image.

# 1 INTRODUCTION

During the time I was working for the Ministry of Natural Resources (1966 to 1996), I made a list of all the fishes I found in Lake Nipissing. Since my retirement, I have found my list of fish species on several websites. The Ministry of Natural Resources claimed it as their property since I developed the list during my work career. People use it as common knowledge which indeed it is now.

The main body of this book consists of detailed descriptions of the fishes found in Lake Nipissing. In the beginning I describe the birth of Lake Nipissing. Because of this beginning of the lake, there seemed to be something missing. After all, Lake Nipissing and its fishes are deeply associated with people. Therefore, I describe the first coming of humans to the Americas. These two topics, associated with the lake, have held my interest over a long period of time.

## 2 THE ICE AGE

During the last 2.3 million years ice ages came and went. The ice sheet from the most recent event reached its maximum 18,000 years ago. The ice at the glacial maximum was 2 km. thick. The weight of the ice compressed the earth causing the land to sink. The compression also caused the land to buckle and rise in some locations.

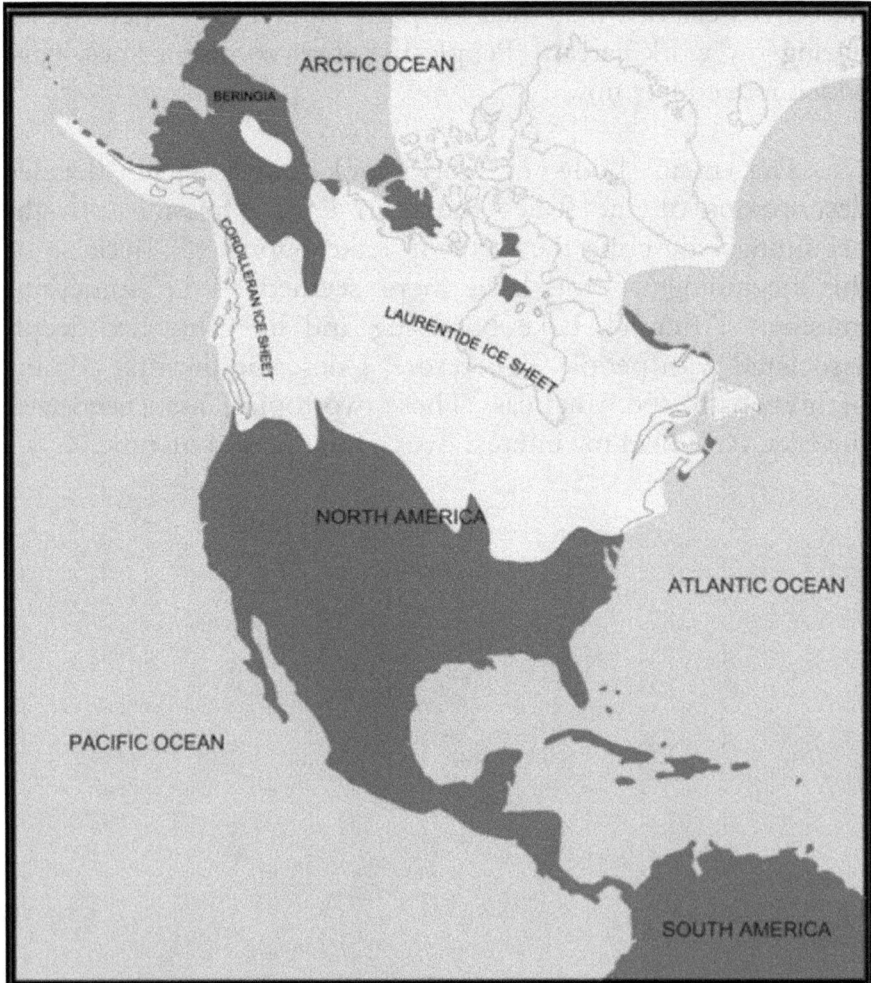

*18,000 years ago the glaciation of North America reached its maximum.*

The snow which formed the glaciers came from the ocean. It is estimated that 50 to 60 million cubic kilometers of ocean water went into forming the ice age glaciers. This caused the ocean water levels to drop 121 metres. The weight of the water in the oceans therefore decreased which caused some of the sea bottom to rise due to the decreased pressure. Therefore, coastal areas were extended and what is called land bridges appeared on various parts of the planet. One of these effects was that it was possible at this time to walk from what is now France to England over what eventually became the English Channel. Another effect was the formation of a land bridge between Asia and Alaska, called Beringia.

People of what is called the Clovis culture came from Asia

across the Bering land bridge (Beringia) approximately 12,000 years ago and populated the Americas.

NO! They could not get past the 2 km. high glacier. But this was the paleo archeological theory for over one hundred years.

Archaeologists found a mammoth killed in Washington State well before the arrival of the Clovis people. The mastodon had a spear point imbeded in one of the bones. The spear point was not made by Clovis people.

Archaeologists dug up a campsite in southern Chile close to the tip of South America. The camp site was dated to about 14,600 years ago. This is more than 1,000 years before the oldest known Clovis tools.

Pre-Clovis style artefacts have been found in Texas. Humans lived on California's Channel Islands 12,000 years ago. There were migrations from Europe across the Atlantic 16,500 years ago.

Many Native Americans have ancient stories and legends about their first arrival in America. They talk about coming by boats and ships. Geneticists then became interested in the Native American origins. Comparisons of DNA from fossil finds were made with today's Native Americans. One genetic marker used was Haplo Group X. This marker comes from western Europeans, not Asians. The most frequent occurrence of Haplo Group X is in the Algonquin speaking tribes, e.g., Ojibwa. Haplo Group X entered America about 30,000 years ago.

It was found that Blackfoot, Iroquois and other tribes from Minnesota, Michigan, Massachusetts and Ontario are descended from the Jomon. The Jomon existed in Japan's Neolithic age from about 10,000 B.C. To 300 B.C. They were not Mongoloids from China or Korea. They were Caucasians. The remnants of this lost Caucasian race, called Ainu, live mostly in Hokkaido.

Helsiuk's oral history mention Triquet Island on B.C.'s Central Coast. B.C. archaeologists have excavated a settlement in the area — in traditional Heiltsuk Nation territory — and dated it to 14,000 years ago, during the last ice age before the Clovis people entered North America.

In Canada's Yukon Territory is a place called Bluefish Caves consisting of three caves. Along with evidence of human habitation, horse remains were found in Bluefish Caves dating to 24,000 years ago.

The Clovis people who entered the north of America via the Bering land bridge 12,000 years ago became trapped on Beringia where they hunted mastodon and giant bison. About 10,000 years ago the ice sheets began to melt. The mastodon and giant bison became extinct. The Clovis people on Beringia walked into the north of North America and eventually became the Inuit.

As the ice sheets melt water rushed back into the oceans, the water levels rose back to the original levels. The bottom areas which had risen during the glacial period sank again under the tens of thousands of tons of water added to the oceans. The land bridges disappeared and the English Channel was back in place.

The melt water could not find it's way back into the oceans right away. A lot of water was trapped on the land and formed huge lakes. One of these lakes was Lake Agassiz which covered areas in Ontario, Manitoba and Saskatchewan.

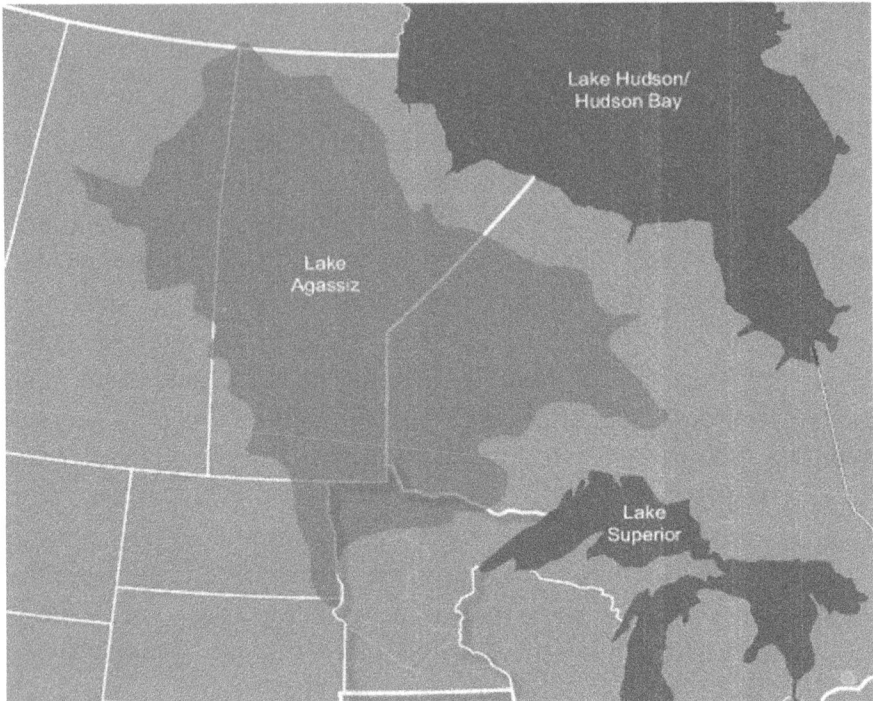

*Lake Agassiz formed at the end of the last glaciation period.*

Other huge lakes which formed were Glacial Lake Algonquin and Glacial Lake Iroquois. Lake Algonquin covered a large area and eventually formed the upper Great Lakes. The huge ice sheets had gouged deep impressions into the earth. These glacier depressions became lakes when they filled with melt water. The huge gouges where Lake Iroquois was formed eventually formed quite a few lakes. One of these was Lake Ontario. As the glacier kept melting there eventually formed Lake Nipissing north of Lake Ontario.

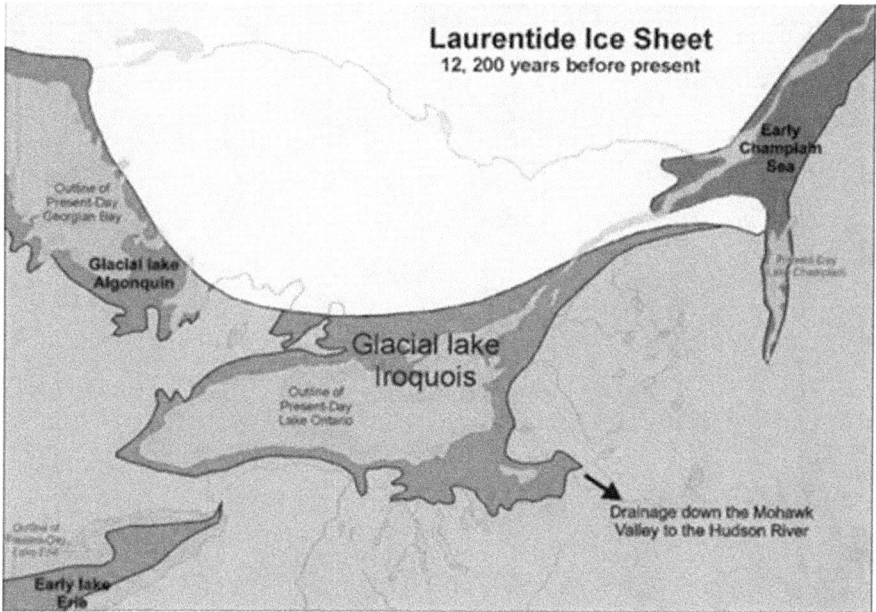

*Lakes Algonquin and Iroquis 12,200 years ago*

As the terrific weight of the glaciers decreased during the melting process, the compressed land slowly rebounded. Over a long period of time this made much of the water in the huge lakes rush to the ocean. Thus were created the Great Lakes (and Lake Nipissing). The land rebounded very slowly. It still rebounds today at a rate of about one centimeter per year.

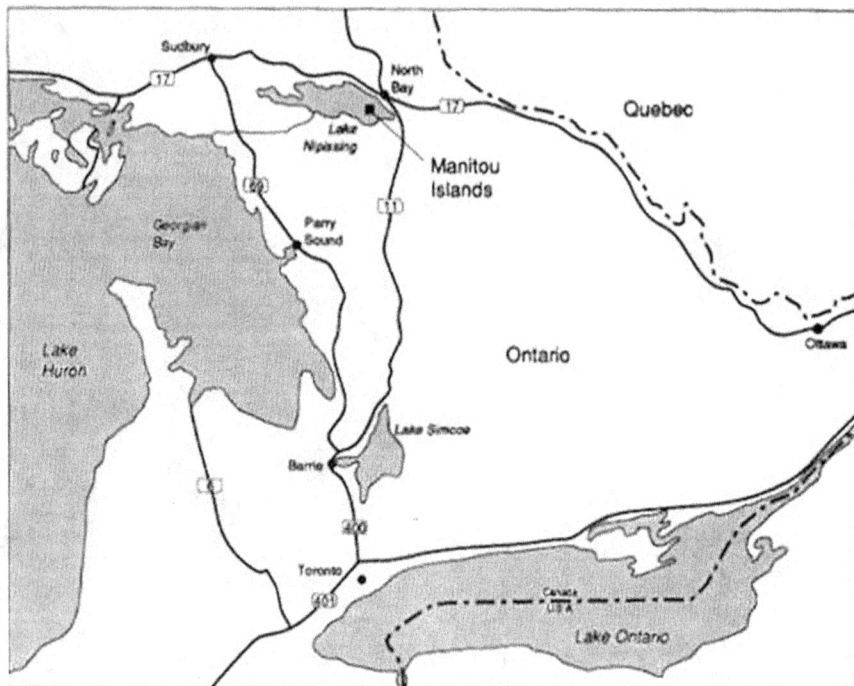

*Eventually Lake Nipissing was formed north of Lake Ontario.*

As pressure was released from the earth, seismic pressure formed deep in the earth which caused earth quakes and volcanic activity. Two volcanoes erupted on Lake Nipissing. The Manitou Islands are the lip of a volcanic pipe attached to a deep origin volcano.

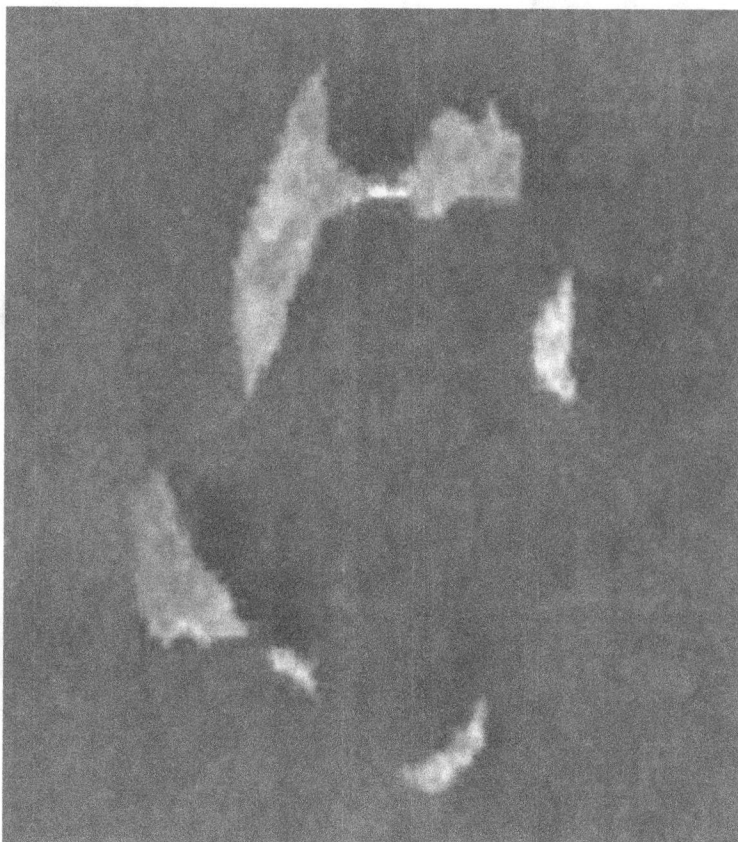

*The Manitou Islands are the exposed rim of a sunken volcano.*

Another exposed rim of a volcano that we can see today is called Callander Bay.

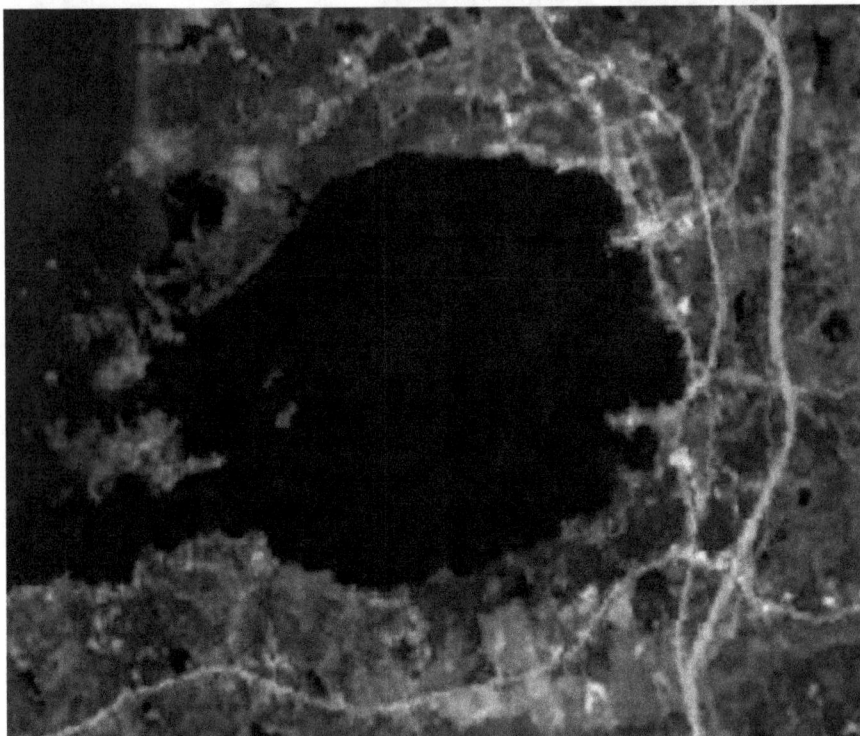

*Satellite picture of Callander Bay. It is the top of a volcanic pipe attached to a deep origin volcano.*

# 3 THE FISHES

During my career as the Lake Nipissing Fisheries Biologist I made a list of all the species of fish that I found in Lake Nipissing. The list is presented here:

## List of fish species in lake Nipissing

Walleye (yellow pickerel)

Yellow Perch

Great Northern Pike

Muskellunge (maskinonge)

Lake Sturgeon

Common Garpike

Common Whitefish

Cisco

Rainbow Smelt

Lake Trout

Speckled Trout

Rainbow Trout

Common White Sucker

Redhorse Sucker

Brown Bullhead (catfish)

Channel Catfish

Pumpkinseed Sunfish

Bluegill Sunfish

Rock Bass

Large-mouth Bass

Small-mouth Bass

White Bass

Sheepshead

Burbot (Ling)

Golden Shiner

Northern Common Shiner

Fine Scaled Dace

Straw-coloured Minnow

Spot-tailed Minnow

Lake Shiner

Blunt-nosed Minnow

Lake Chub

Fathead Minnow

Redbelly Dace

Mud Minnow

Trout Perch

Nine Spined Stickleback

Log Perch

Johnny Darter

Iowa Darter

Eastern Slimy Sculpin

Northern Mottled Sculpin

Silver Lamprey

# 4 WALLEYE (YELLOW PICKEREL)

Walleye have many common names. They are called pickerel or yellow pickerel by English Canadians. The French Canadiens call them Dore. The scientific name used to be *Stizostedion vitreum vitreum* Mitchill. (Mitchill is the name of the biologist who classified this species and gave it its name). The scientific name has now been changed to *Sander vitreus.*

The walleye is a member of the Perch family (Percidae). The other members of the Percidae are the common yellow perch, the saugers and the darters. These fish are called spiny-rayed fishes. This is because they have stiff, sharp spines in their dorsal, anal and pectoral fins.

In Lake Nipissing, walleye spawn in the spring when the water temperatures are between 3.33° C and 6.7° C. This takes place at night usually around April 25, but may vary quite a bit. Large numbers of walleye ascend tributary streams. Spawning also takes place at some of the islands in the lake. The male walleye first time spawners arrive first. A few days later the females show up and spawning commences. Later, the large experienced spawners arrive at the spawning locations. The eggs are sticky and adhere to the bottom gravel and boulders so that the water current does not sweep them away to an unfavourable place.

These fish do not eat when spawning. Therefore, just after the spawning season they are ravenous and easy to catch on a hook and line. Many tourists come to Lake Nipissing at this time of year.

In Lake Nipissing the walleye is the top predator. Their favourite food is yellow perch. However, any bite sized fish will do. They even eat smaller walleye. Big fish eat little fish. The position as top predator (the apex predator) means that the walleye controls the eco-system of the lake by preventing the pan fish population from becoming overabundant and stunted. If the population of walleye is over fished, things will happen to all the other fishes. One example is that a smaller population of walleye will leave more forage fish available causing the yellow perch not only to increase in abundance but also to assume the habits of the walleye, which results in increased growth and produces jumbo perch.

## WHERE TO FISH FOR WALLEYE

The walleye form themselves into schools according to their size. These schools then hunt along the shoreline. A walleye school may be compared to a pack of wolves when hunting. They chase down their prey. In light of this behaviour, the best success for finding walleye is along the shoreline, especially where the land forms a point jutting into the lake. Often good fishing may be had along the islands in Lake Nipissing.

# 5 YELLOW PERCH

The yellow perch is a member of the Perch family (Percidae). The other members of the Percidae are the walleye (yellow pickerel), the saugers and the darters. These fish are called spiny-rayed fishes. This is because they have stiff, sharp spines in their dorsal, anal and pectoral fins.

The perch are sexually mature at the age of two and during the months of April and May, spawning takes place in sheltered areas at night in water five to ten feet in depth. They spawn when the water temperature is between 7° C and 10° C. Gelatinous strings of eggs are released freely in the water and the males quickly fertilize them. The spawn become attached to aquatic vegetation or submerged brush or gravel or even sand. The eggs hatch in twelve to twenty-one days.

## WHERE TO FISH FOR YELLOW PERCH

The yellow perch are most numerous in expanses of open water, with moderate amounts of vegetation. They often swim in loose schools in large numbers. They prefer a temperature of 21° C. Their favourite food are copepods and cladocerans (water fleas). Perch also feed on aquatic insects, crayfish, snails, and fishes such as minnows, sucker, herring, sunfish, and stickleback. Therefore, live bait works very well.

# 6 GREAT NORTHERN PIKE

The Latin or scientific name of the great northern pike is *Esox lucius* Linnaeus. It is a member of the family Esocidae. This family includes the pikes, the true pickerels, and the maskinonge. The pike has an elongated, somewhat compressed body. There is a single dorsal fin placed far back near the tail. There are no spines in the fins.

The pike becomes sexually mature at the age of three. As the ice melts along the shore, the pike move to their spawning grounds. If there is sufficient melt water at this time, the pike will move into drainage ditches, flooded grassy margins of lakes and even flooded pastures. The larger female is accompanied by one or more males and eggs are deposited on vegetation in water four to eighteen inches deep.

## WHERE TO FISH FOR GREAT NORTHERN PIKE

In the spring and summer, the pike prefers weedy bays, estuaries and shoals. As the walleye were compared to a pack of wolves when hunting, the great northern pike may be compared to a cat. The pike hides in the vegetation until a suitable prey comes along. Then, when the prey is close enough, the pike swoops out and catches its prey. If the prey did not come close enough, the pike will gradually sneak up on it like a cat and when it is close enough it will pounce. Their preferred food are perch, shiners, and young pan fish. Sometimes a pike will eat a muskrat, a duckling or a frog. Occasionally a northern pike will leap out of the water to catch and eat a small low flying bird (e.g., a swallow)

# 7 MASKINONGE

The Latin or scientific name of the maskinonge is *Esox masquinongy* Mitchill. Like the great northern pike it is a member of the family Esocidae. Many people call this fish muskellunge. Some use a pet name and call it a "musky". The maskinonge has an elongated, somewhat compressed body. There is a single dorsal fin placed far back near the tail. There are no spines in the fins. The cheeks and opercles (membrane bones located behind the cheeks and covering the gills) are scaled on the upper half and the lower halves are naked. In the pike, the cheeks are entirely scaled and the opercles are scaled above but the lower half is naked. The other distinction between the maskinonge and the pike is the colour of the fish. The pike is more of a green colour and the maskinonge is more of a blue colour.

Spawning takes place early in the spring when the water temperature is 9.5° C. When spawning the maskinonge swim around in pairs, side by side, keeping the same position while turning, going under logs, etc. They seem almost to be cemented together. The eggs and milt are scattered at random in very shallow water (15 to 20 inches deep).

# WHERE TO FISH FOR MASKINONGE

Maskinonge hunt their prey similarly to that of the great northern pike. They have been caught in the West Bay of Lake Nipissing. During my explorations in West Bay, the fishing guides were telling stories about one very large maskinonge who had become very famous. Many anglers when they have caught a fish, will put the fish on a stringer (wire, or chain often with snaps on which fish are strung by a fisherman) and keep the caught fish at the side of the boat in the lake by means of this stringer. The infamous, huge, maskinonge made it a habit of swimming up to the fishing boats and stealing the fish attached to the stringers. Maskinonge weighing 30 to 40 pounds are not unusual.

# 8 LAKE STURGEON

The scientific name of this fish is *Acipenser fulvescens* Refinesque. It is the largest of the native fishes of Ontario. The colour is slate-grey on top and paler on the underside. The skeleton is cartilage. The young are tan or buff coloured with large blotches on the sides. This fish has no teeth.

Sturgeon males are mature at age 14 and females at age 23. In the latter part of May or early June the sturgeon enter the Sturgeon River to spawn. Once, at the approach of the spawning season, I saw a big sturgeon jump vertically right out of the water about five feet from my boat. They spawn in about ten feet of water on stony or gravelly bottom close to rapids or waterfalls.

## FISHING FOR STURGEON

The sturgeon has four barbels in front of the mouth which helps it to locate food. They feed on the bottom. Their sucker mouth has no teeth so they suck up their food which consists of mayfly nymphs, chironomid larvae (midge fly larvae), molluscs, stonefly larvae, dragon fly nymphs, crayfish and other crustacea.

The lake sturgeon can reach a length of eight feet and a weight of 300 pounds or more. People do not angle for sturgeon. While fishing for walleye, the angler lowers his baited hook to the bottom and then pulls it up about a foot or two. Occasionally an angler has let his hook sink to the bottom where a big lake sturgeon has swallowed the lure. An angler who is unable to land the fish, instead gets towed in his boat all the way across Lake Nipissing by the sturgeon.

# 9 COMMON GARPIKE

The common garpike is also known as the billfish or longnose gar. The scientific name is *Lepisosteus osseus* Linnaeus. The body is very elongated and sub-cylindrical. The body is covered with obliquely and regularly diamond shaped hard plates or scales. The plates are covered with an enamel like substance called ganoin. The skin is therefore extremely tough. It is so tough that pioneers used to cover their wooden plough shares with the skin from the garpike.

The body length may reach five feet and three foot individuals are common. The jaws are elongated into a beak which is twice as long as the head. These jaws have several rows of teeth which are exceptionally strong, sharp, and conical. The colour of these fish vary but are greenish above, silvery on the sides and white below. The body and fins have large black spots or blotches. The skeleton is part cartilage and part bone. One strange feature is that the swim bladder is connected to the pharynx. This may therefore be used as a lung. They can rise to the surface, expel air from the air bladder and take in a fresh supply. The fish also has normal gills, but the pharynx air bladder arrangement enables this fish to live in water with extremely low oxygen content.

The garpike spawns in late spring or early summer. They spawn in large schools in close formation. The eggs are deposited in shallow weedy bays on submerged vegetation or aquatic plant roots. The eggs are small and dark in colour.

These eggs are poisonous for terrestrial animals, but not to fish.

Garpike eat crayfish and insects but it prefers to eat fish. They eat game fish, panfish, minnows, darters, troutperch and killifish. I have seen them only in the West Bay of Lake Nipissing. There they float on the surface resembling floating logs. Thus they wait for a fish to come near so that they can grab them and eat them.

## 10 COMMON WHITEFISH

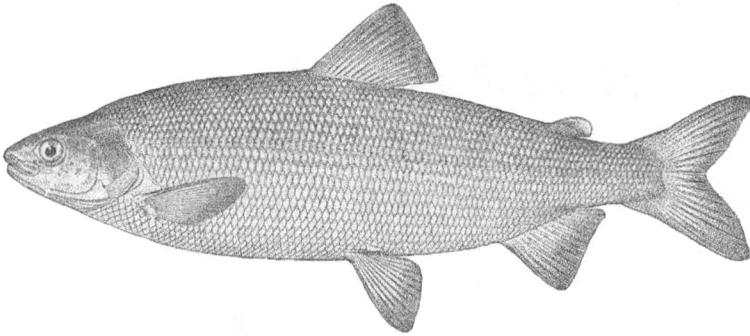

The common whitefish is also called the Great Lakes whitefish and lake whitefish. The scientific name is *Coregonus clupeaformis* Mitchill. The body of the whitefish is deep and laterally compressed. The colour is silvery and the scales are large and easily removed. Anglers often mistake cisco for whitefish, however when in doubt, a simple examination of the fish will enable an angler to positively identify his catch as either cisco or whitefish. The rounded, blunt snout of the whitefish distinctly overhangs the lower jaw. The mouth of the cisco is an angular profile. Whitefish are an important part of the Ontario commercial fishing industry.

Whitefish mature at three to five years old and spawn in October and November when the shoal waters have cooled.

Basically considered to be bottom feeders, the whitefish feed on small molluscs, aquatic insect larvae, and small fishes. The whitefish is found in the shoal waters most of the year, dispersing to deeper waters only as the shallow water becomes warmer during the summer months. The average depth of Lake Nipissing is fifteen feet. About one-half of one percent of the lake is over 75 feet deep. The deeper waters are found at the source of the French River (incorrectly called the mouth of the French by many people). There the water depth goes down to 150 feet. In some places on the French River the depth goes below 300 feet.

## WHERE TO FISH FOR WHITEFISH

Lake Nipissing can provide excellent recreational fishing for whitefish. Winter whitefish angling on Lake Nipissing is usually conducted in water 15 ft. to 40 ft. in depth. The most heavily fished areas for whitefish on Lake Nipissing are Callander Bay, Deepwater Point, and South Bay. Prospective whitefish anglers should keep in mind that Lake Nipissing is large and much of the lake will likely produce whitefish if the angler has a desire to search for new areas. In the summer the whitefish angler will fish in the cooler deep water of the lake and during the fall the shallow water and the mouth of the Sturgeon River are considered likely whitefish angling grounds.

Winter whitefish anglers pre-bait their fishing area with salted minnows. Although not often used on Lake Nipissing, cooked rice, wheat or other grains may also be utilized to attract whitefish. After pre-baiting the fishing area, anglers use special spreader rigs baited with small minnows. Anglers fish well into the evening and good catches of whitefish from 4 lbs. to 9 lbs. are not uncommon.

# 11 CISCO

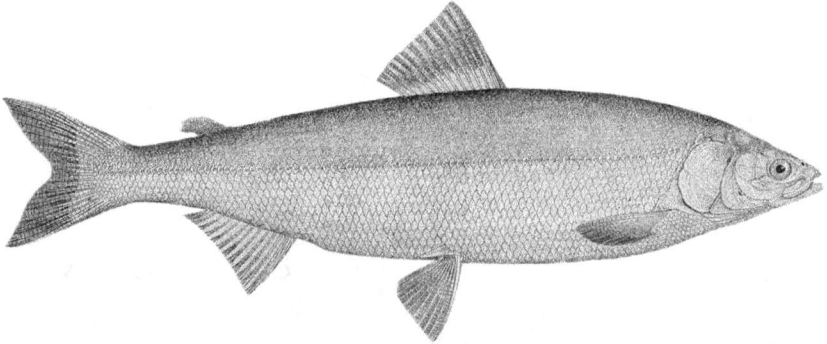

The cisco of Lake Nipissing is most commonly called lake herring. It is also called tullibee, ciscoe, blueback, shallow-water cisco and greyback tullibee. The French common name is cisco de lac. The scientific name is *Coregonus artedii* Le Sueur.

The cisco is laterally compressed. The mouth is by the front of the head and is not overhung by the snout as in the whitefish. It has large silvery eyes. The back varies from a dark blue to a pale gray-green. The sides are silvery. The pectoral fins are clear and the pelvic and anal fins slightly white. All three fins have traces of black colouring on the tips.

The ciscoes bear a superficial resemblance to the true marine herrings, but they are not close relatives of these latter fishes.

Spawning is usually underway on sandy and gravelly shoals as ice starts to form.

In late spring and early summer the cisco leave the shallower water and migrate into the colder deeper water. Cisco feed on bottom dwelling organisms, crustaceans and fresh water shrimp. The fry of some other fish are also sometimes eaten.

## WHERE TO FISH FOR CISCO

In the spring when the ice leaves the lake, the ciscoes are almost uniformly distributed over the lake, being somewhat more abundant in the shallower parts.

With the onset of summer, the surface and the shallow water of the lake becomes warmed. As summer advances, the warm water extends deeper and the shallow and surface water reaches higher temperatures.

The ciscoes can not live in regions of the lake in which the water has been warmed, so they gradually move into deeper water as the shallow water increases in temperature.

When the ciscoes have reached the area adjacent to or at the deepest part, they are living at a depth of about 30 feet below the surface.

Finally, the temperature at this depth becomes so warm that the cisco do not care for food. They swim through the thermocline into the deep cold region of the French River area.

When the fish go into this cold region, they do not recover from the temperature shock immediately. It is often three or four weeks before they start to feed again. In the fall the water cools again and the cisco come up and disperse to all areas of the lake where they remain during the winter.

It is during the fall and spring that ciscoes are most readily caught.

The cisco is a fly-taker during its spring and autumn period in the shoal water, and is gamey on a light fly rod. Through the summer, deep trolling with small spinners and still fishing with various baits are effective. Like the whitefish, the cisco is good winter game for ice fishermen and similar angling methods are very effective in certain areas.

For spring and fall fishing such bait as mayflies, small live or salted minnows, or artificial lures such as flashy pearl buttons and small coloured baits have proven to be successful.

# 12 RAINBOW SMELT

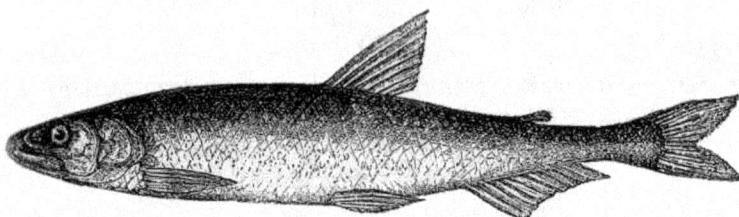

It is claimed that the name smelt is a contraction of the words "smell it", this reference being to the fish's peculiar odour which is not unlike that of fresh cucumbers. The scientific name is *Osmerus mordax* Mitchill.

The smelt is a slender, silvery fish, pale green on the back and with purple, blue and pink iridescence on the sides. Spawning males have small tubercles scattered over the head and body.

## WHERE TO FISH FOR SMELT

Smelt are schooling fish that generally inhabit the offshore areas of lakes. Shortly after ice out in the spring, they begin to ascend streams to spawn. Spawning may last as long as 3 weeks but usually the peak is less than a week. It is during this period that smelt are most vulnerable to fishermen.

In the Great Lakes area the annual spring run of smelt is greeted by a horde of would be smelt fishermen using equipment ranging from bare hands to 30 foot seines. Dip nets made of fine wire mesh are most commonly used. Other necessary equipment includes a large container for the fish and wood and a fry pan for cooking fish fresh from the water. Dip nets may not be larger than 6 feet square and seine nets can not be larger than 30 feet.

Smelt are also taken by angling through the ice in some inland lakes. Fishing is done over deep waters, but the fish may be swimming at any depth. Usually a group of fishermen fish together and set all of their lines at different depths. When the depth at which fish are feeding is located, all lines are set at that depth. Bait is usually a small shiner minnow placed on the hooks of a very small spoon. Because the smelt bite lightly, the line must be supported by a sensitive wire or tip-up such as that used for whitefish.

In many waters, the best bait is a strip cut from the smelt itself near the tail. Other baits are bits of smelt skin, perch skin, live minnows, and brightly coloured fins.

# 13 LAKE TROUT

The scientific name of lake trout is *Salvelinus namaycush* Walbaum. It is one of the fishes known as char which includes the brook trout and the Dolly Varden trout. The scales of the lake trout are very small and are imbeded in the skin to such a degree that they often escape notice. The body is elongated, the head large, and the tail deeply forked. The colour varies quite a bit and may be greyish, greenish, brownish or blackish. There are numerous pale or light-coloured spots on the back, sides, cheeks, gillcovers, and dorsal and tail fins.

Lake trout spawn on rocky reefs or shoals. They enter the spawning grounds when the water temperature is 14° C. Spawning takes place when the water temperature is between 14° C and 6.6° C. At a minimum depth of two feet, when there is a strong wind causing wave action. They may spawn at a depth of up to ten feet.

Lake trout feed on whitefish, cisco, smelt, and ling. When forage fish are not available, they feed on plankton.

## WHERE TO FISH FOR LAKE TROUT

The lake trout are found in the French River in depths of 200 to 300 feet.

*Author Carsten R. Jorgensen holding a Lake Trout*

# 14 SPECKLED TROUT

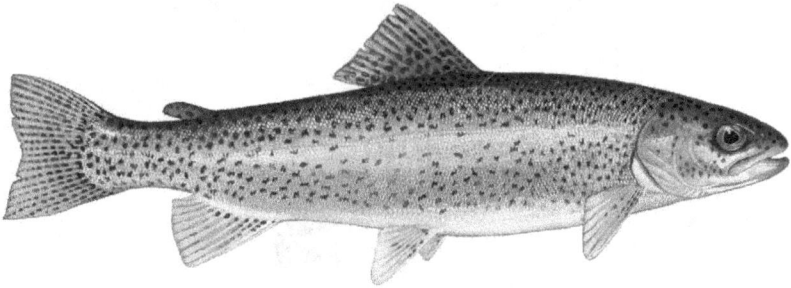

The speckled trout is often called brook trout. The scientific name is *Salvelinus fontinales* Mitchill.

This trout is an unusually beautiful fish. It is usually olive green, darker on the back and lighter on the sides. The sides are marked with numerous rounded red spots with blue borders. The lower part of the sides are pinkish and the belly is white. There are wavy, dark green, worm like markings on the back. The scales are very small and sometimes escape notice.

Speckled trout spawn in the last three months of the year. The female builds a nest with the help of the male. She fans out the nest in the gravel of the stream by swimming on her side and moving her head and tail up and down very fast. The eggs are then laid and fertilized by the male. The eggs are sticky and cling to the inside of the nest.

Speckled trout feed mainly on insects. Food consists of immature mayflies, caddisflies and two-winged flies such as crane flies, horse flies, and blue bottle flies. Large fish also feed on minnows, crayfish and other crustaceans. Their preferred temperature is 20° C to 24° C.

## WHERE TO FISH FOR SPECKLED TROUT

Speckled trout live in streams running into Lake Nipissing. Although they sometimes enter the lake, they do not go far from their home stream. Fishing will not be successful in the lake. Successful fishing is carried out in the creeks where they are found.

There used to be speckled trout in Duchesney Creek. In my book "TRYING TO WORK FOR THE M.N.R." I wrote:

"In the past, there had been walleye spawning at the mouth of Duchesney Creek. Chemical tests at the mouth of Duchesney Creek showed that the water there was acidic with a pH of 4 and unsuitable for fish. My research on Duchesney Creek revealed that not only did walleye used to spawn at the mouth of the creek but there used to be brook trout in the creek itself.

There was a John Mansville plant on Duchesney Creek which I suspected of causing the acidic water. I called John Mansville on the phone and asked them what was in the effluent which they discharged. The person on the line refused to speak with me. I drove to the plant to talk with them. I was shown into an office where a very nice gentleman was sitting behind a desk and he invited me to sit down. We had a great conversation. The gentleman said that they had no effluents going into the creek. Their waste products were collected and loaded onto trucks and were driven away.

I then had my casual biologist do chemical testing above the John Mansville plant. He found the acid to be just as bad above the plant. This verified that the effluent did not come from the John Mansville plant. My casual biologist tested water further and further north on Duchesney Creek. We discovered that the acidic water actually came from the Psychiatric Hospital. The acid pollution stopped when the Psychiatric Hospital closed.

Water quality was not my responsibility. This was the responsibility of the Ministry of the Environment. Much later, (2016) I discovered that the Psychiatric Hospital had not been on city sewer and water services. An internet web site stated: 'In 2011 it was stated that to extend sewer and water from North Bay to the site would cost $15 M.'

I suspect that the sewage effluents were treated with some kind of acid to kill the bacteria and smell, thus causing pollution in Duchesney Creek."

One of the ways in which hatcheries may be a useful tool in fisheries management is to stock fish in suitable new waters. I do not know whether the M.N.R has stocked speckled trout into Duchesney Creek since the Psychiatric hospital closed."

# 15 RAINBOW TROUT

The scientific name of the rainbow trout is *Salmo gairdneri* Richardson. Rainbow trout are very variable in colour, spotting, body form, and other characteristics. Because of this, taxonomists considered them to be a number of separate and distinct species. But it was discovered that the variations were due to environmental differences in their habitats. With time, rainbows acquire characteristics of resident populations in any body of water.

The body of the rainbow trout is trout like, spindle shaped, and laterally compressed. The larger fish are deep-bodied. The colour varies with the environment. The back may be bluish, bluish green, greenish, or olive green on the back. It is silvery on the sides and light below. A pink lateral band of variable width runs from behind the eye to the end of the tail. This band is redder or reddish purple on mature fish.

Rainbow trout are native in the Pacific Ocean from south Alaska to Mexico. From 1880 to 1895, rainbow trout were propagated and raised in the east from rainbows living in the McCloud River, a tributary of the Sacramento River in California. In 1883, the Provincial Government imported rainbow trout from the McCloud River and planted them near Sault Ste. Marie.

Rainbow trout are now widely distributed in numerous lakes and streams in the Great Lakes watershed. Their preferred temperature is 5° C to 13° C.

Important food for the rainbow are aquatic insects; specially may flies, caddis flies, black flies and stone flies. They also eat leaf hoppers, grasshoppers, true bugs, leeches, and crayfish.

Spawning begins in mid-November and ceases in January. The female scoops out a depression four to five inches deep and 15 inches wide. When the eggs are laid, they are immediately fertilized by the male and covered with gravel by the female. This takes only a few seconds.

## WHERE TO FISH FOR RAINBOW TROUT

Rainbow remain near river mouths during the winter and enter the streams with the first spring floods. In Lake Nipissing they are not found in the main lake. They inhabit the French River portion. Because they leave the lake to ascend the tributaries, they are caught in smaller lakes close to the French River.

# 16 COMMON WHITE SUCKER

The scientific name of the common white sucker is *Catostomus commersoni* Lacepede. The white sucker has an elongated and robust body. The sucker-like mouth is overhung by the snout and is directed downwards. The lips are thick with the upper lip thinner than the lower. The fins are large and dusky. The back is dark, almost black, shading to silvery on the sides.

The white sucker spawns in streams with moderate to swift rifles. Eggs are laid in gravelly or stony areas in April or May when the water temperature is above 4° C. When following walleye to their spawning beds in the spring time, they come themselves to spawn and at that time do not feed.

Suckers are bottom feeders eating such food as midge fly larvae, caddis fly larvae and molluscs. Water-fleas constitute 60 to 90% of the food of many individuals in the summer. Active feeding is usually restricted to near sunrise and sunset when they move into shallower water. But they remain moderately active during the daytime.

## WHERE TO FISH FOR SUCKERS

Suckers are found throughout the lake. Angling for suckers with light tackle is an interesting pastime. The gear necessary is simple. Consisting of pole, line, light leader, split shot sinker, and a single hook, number 6 or number 8. A variety of baits may be used, such as grubs, worms, and night crawlers. Other popular baits include dough balls, small spinners, and wet flies.

White suckers are most vulnerable during the spring spawning run, when they are not only taken by angling gear, but may be taken with a spear during the daytime in April and May, and with a dip-net during daylight hours in March, April, and May in the Lake Nipissing area.

*The sucker-like mouth is overhung by the snout and is directed downwards.*

# 17 REDHORSE SUCKER

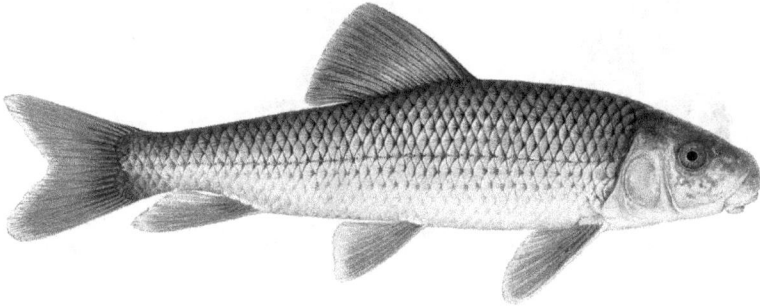

The scientific name of the redhorse sucker is *Moxostoma carinatum* Cope.

The body of the redhorse is deeper than it is wide. The mouth small and sucker-like and directed downwards. The back is olive green shading to pale green on the sides. The fins are reddish.

Like the white sucker, redhorse are bottom feeders eating such food as midge fly larvae, caddis fly larvae and molluscs. Water-fleas constitute 60 to 90% of the food of many individuals in summer. Active feeding is usually restricted to near sunrise and sunset when they move into shallower water. But they remain moderately active during the daytime.

# 18 BROWN BULLHEAD

The brown bullhead is often referred to as a mud cat, horned pout, barbotte, and most often as a catfish. Its scientific name is *Ictalurus nebulosus* Le Sueur.

The brown bullhead is usually 8 to 14 inches in length and weighs less than a pound. The brown bullhead is best described as a stocky fish with a slippery scaleless skin, ranging in colour from olive to dark brown. The mouth is large and wide with eight barbels, more often referred to by anglers as whiskers. It may be the whiskered appearance of the fish that resulted in the name "catfish". Young catfish anglers are quick to remind newcomers to the fraternity that the whiskers will cut unwary fingers. This is not true; however, the spines in the dorsal and pectoral fins are pointed and the fish should be handled with care.

The brown bullheads spawn in April to June. Both the male and female use their spiny fins to excavate a slight depression, eight inches to one foot wide, in shallow water near aquatic weeds at the edge of a bank, or under a log or stump. They also use the mouths of muskrat burrows or natural depressions. The amber coloured eggs are produced in gelatinous masses about three inches in diameter. They usually produce 6,000 to 13,000 eggs. Both parents guard the eggs. In eight to ten days the babies hatch. When the babies leave the nest, both parents accompany them. One remains in the immediate vicinity. The other is some distance away to watch for enemies.

The brown bullhead is a bottom feeder. The long sensory barbels on their chin helps to assist them in locating their food which consists of aquatic insect larvae, crayfish, molluscs, and occasionally fish and plant material. The spinous processes in their fins are their defence. Because of these fins, they have partial immunity. I have on two occasions been wounded by a brown bullhead when I tried to take one from a line. As my hand reached for it, the fish shook itself violently and the spine entered my hand into the flesh between my thumb and forefinger. It was very painful.

## WHERE TO FISH FOR BROWN BULLHEAD

In Lake Nipissing the brown bullheads usually occur near the bottom in shallow water with abundant aquatic vegetation and sand to mud floors. Favourite angling locations include Cache Bay, weedy areas of West Bay, the Lavigne areas, the West Arm weedy areas, Callander Bay, and South Bay. They are largely nocturnal but they will feed in early morning and during the day when it is cloudy.

This species is not covered by seasons, or bag limits and could provide anglers with enjoyment and food prior to the opening of the season for more restricted sport fish. Bullheads feed on or near the bottom, mainly at night. For this reason bullheads bite best at night and the baited hook should rest right on the bottom.

Although worms are favoured as bait by most brown bullhead anglers, the brown bullhead is omnivorous and will eat almost anything. Their food is composed of molluscs, immature insects, terrestrial insects, leeches, crustaceans (crayfish and plankton), worms, algae, plant material, fishes, and fish eggs. Some anglers bait their hook and line with bait such as corn, hellgrammites, crayfish, blood bait, dough balls, and even chunks of laundry soap. Baits that emit an odour are especially effective because the food is searched out largely by means of the barbels, and by the means of "taste" and "smell".

Boat fishermen use a cane pole, eight to ten feet in length with an equal length of line. However, this is optional. Some use only hook and line which is equal to any rod and reel when bottom fishing in relatively shallow water. It is extremely important to bring lots of extra hooks because bullheads may take the bait so deep that it is easier to cut the line than remove the hook. The following catfish bait recipe has been highly recommended:

Mix one cup of flour, one cup of corn meal and ten tablespoons of thick molasses. Stir into stiff dough and roll into bait balls. Drop into boiling water, Boil ten minutes. Remove and drop into cold water. This bait stays on the hook.

# 19 CHANNEL CATFISH

The scientific name of the channel catfish is *Ictalurus punctatus* Rafinesque. It is the most trimly built of all the catfishes. Like the brown bullhead they have strong sharp spines in their dorsal and ventral fins. The colour varies quite a bit. It might be light silvery grey or bluish green and a paler silver below. It could also be olivaceous or slate coloured above and silvery to white below. The body has small, scattered, dark spots. It is easily distinguished from the other species of catfish by its forked tail.

Spawning takes place in obscure places such as horizontal burrows, crevices, overhanging rock ledges, undercut banks, and hollow logs. They spawn when the water temperature reaches 24° C. The male catfish guards the eggs until they hatch. Then, he watches over the newly hatched fry for a short time.

Channel catfish are active swimmers and are piscivorous eating minnows, perch and other fish of suitable size. Although eating mainly fish, they will also eat crayfish, earthworms and insects. This fish may reach a weight of 30 pounds or more.

There are no channel catfish in the main part of Lake Nipissing. While I was working as the Lake Nipissing biologist I heard of channel catfish in the French River. However, I have been unable to verify it at this time. Consequently I am unable to state where to fish for this species. On checking the web pages of tourist outfitters on the French River, the sites state that they do not cater to channel catfish anglers. Therefore, if there are channel catfish in this part of Lake Nipissing they are extremely rare.

# 20 SUNFISH

The sunfish are a family of, generally speaking, small to moderately-sized, spiny-rayed, gibbous, laterally-compressed fishes. The eyes are large. The dorsal fin consists of a spiny portion (6-13 spines) and a soft-rayed portion, to a varying degree joined as one fin.

This family is composed of 30 species in 10 genera, and generally grouped as sunfishes, crappies, and basses. The sunfishes found in Lake Nipissing include rock bass, pumpkinseed, and bluegill. These may also be referred to as "pan-fish".

The scientific name of the pumpkinseed is *Lepomis gibbosus* Linnaeus. The pumpkinseed and the bluegill sunfish hybridize extensively. The scientific name of the bluegill is *Lepomis macrochirus.*

The bluegill sunfish also known as blue sunfish, sunfish, bream, and roach have a deep laterally compressed body, small mouth, and a short dark opercular flap. The back is blue-green to olive-green, becoming lighter on the sides and often becoming orange to yellow on the "throat" or "breast". A series of vertical bars may be evident on the sides.

The pumpkinseed also has a laterally compressed body. It is more round in outline than any other sunfish. The mouth is small. The cheeks and opercles have streaks of brilliant blue. A distinguishing feature is the dark opercular flap with a brilliant scarlet spot on the posterior margin. The body is sprinkled with rust coloured scales. Each species reaches a length of from 10 to 12 inches, though the average is about 6 to 8 inches.

Hybrids of bluegill and pumpkinseed are common. The first generation hybrids are capable of spawning.

The rock bass is also laterally compressed but not as markedly as the pumpkinseed and bluegill. The eyes are large and reddish in colour. The body is olive-brown with darker blotches or mottling, the young especially showing conspicuous dark blotches on the sides. With the exception of the pelvic fins, all the fins are dusky and spotted. The scientific name for rock bass is *Ambloplites rupestris* Rafinesque.

Spawning takes place during the latter part of June and into July. The male builds a nest in one to two and a half feet of water. The nest may be twelve to fifteen inches in diameter. Ten to fifteen nests may be constructed in one small area. Eggs are expelled into the nest by one or more than one female. These are fertilized by the male. The male stands guard over the eggs and newly hatched fry, chasing away all intruders.

Sunfish feed mainly on aquatic insects, snails, small crustaceans, leeches, and, occasionally, on the eggs and fry of other fishes.

## WHERE TO FISH FOR SUNFISH

Rock bass, pumpkinseed, and bluegill are found in aggregations and in association with each other throughout the shallow waters of Lake Nipissing. The rock bass, as indicated by its common name, generally prefers rocky areas while the pumpkinseed and bluegill tend to seek out weedy areas. The sunfish are warm water fish and become dormant in the winter.

Rock bass are often found hiding under docks in the summer.

The sunfish have often provided the young angler with his first thrill. It would not be an exaggeration to say that the capture of these sunfish has probably delighted more children than that of any other Canadian fresh water fish.

The rock bass rarely refuses a bait even when offered upon the coarsest of tackle. He bites any time of day or night. The selection of a suitable bait should be easy because of the variety that may be used, for example small minnows, crayfish, hellgramites, crickets, grasshoppers, and worms. Rock bass are often caught when still-fishing or trolling over rocky reefs in lakes using minnows as bait. The use of a live minnow, two inches long, carefully hooked through the lips, lightly cast and allowed to sink to the bottom and slowly reeled in again, is often rewarding. Flies must be allowed to sink with every cast after fluttering them for a while on the surface. Of the artificial lures, the wet or dry fly, small bass bugs, fly and spinner combination are used with considerable success.

There are no closed seasons for rock bass, bluegill or pumpkinseed in this area, so fishing for these delicious pan fish can be enjoyed any time.

# 21 LARGEMOUTH BASS

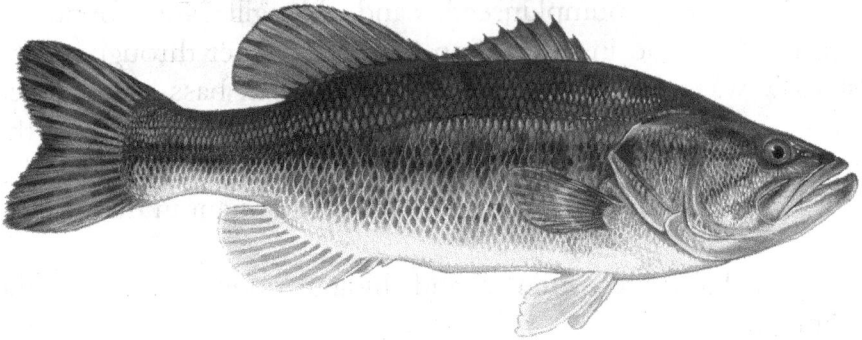

The scientific name of the largemouth bass is *Micropterus salmoides* Lacepede.

The colour of the largemouth bass is mostly bronze-green fading to white below. It may also be dark green over the back, greenish-silvery on the sides, fading to white below. There is a broad dark band of irregular patches on the sides. The upper jaw extends behind the eye when the mouth is closed. In the dorsal fin there are 9 to 10 spines ahead of 12 to 13 soft rays. The dorsal fin is deeply notched, almost completely divided between the spiny part and the soft-rayed part.

The spines in the anal fin usually number three, followed by 10 to 12 soft rays. Six pound fish are not unusual.

When the temperature reaches 15.5° C, usually in May, the male builds a nest six inches deep and two to four feet wide on sand, gravel, clay, or mud bottom. The nest is built in water about three feet in depth. The male coaxes the female into the nest and there the eggs are laid and simultaneously fertilized by the male. The female then leaves the nest. The male remains on guard. He drives away intruders and constantly fans the nest with his fins. The male accompanies the school of fry until the fry reach a length of one inch or more.

Largemouth bass eat worms, mussels, frogs, crayfish, and fish.

## WHERE TO FISH FOR LARGEMOUTH BASS

Largemouth bass feed most actively in the morning and in the evening. They feed near the surface at twilight and in deeper water during the day. They feed close to shore and near weed beds.

# 22 SMALLMOUTH BASS

The scientific name of the smallmouth bass is *Micropterus dolomieui* Lacepede.

The colour of the smallmouth bass is mostly bronze, green, or brownish green and white below. There are dark, bronze coloured vertical bands on the sides. The upper jaw extends to a point between the middle of the pupil and the back of the eye. In the dorsal fin there are 9 to 10 spines ahead of 12 to 13 soft rays. The dorsal fin is deeply notched but not divided between the spiny part and the soft-rayed part.

The spines in the anal fin usually number three, followed by 10 to 12 soft rays. Four pound fish are not unusual, but the average size is one and a half to two and a half pounds

When the temperature reaches 15.5° C, usually in May, the male builds a nest six inches deep and two to four feet wide on sand, or gravel. Smallmouths are unable to spawn on mud. The nest is built in water about three feet in depth. The male coaxes the female into the nest and there the eggs are laid and simultaneously fertilized by the male. The female then leaves the nest. The male remains on guard. He drives away intruders and constantly fans the nest with his fins. The male accompanies the school of fry until the fry reach a length of one inch or more.

Smallmouth bass eat worms, mussels, frogs, crayfish, and fish (perch, darters, sculpins, minnows, suckers, sunfish, and rock bass). Their preferred food is crayfish.

## WHERE TO FISH FOR SMALLMOUTH BASS

Smallmouth bass feed most actively in the morning and in the evening. They feed near the surface at twilight and in deeper water during the day. They feed close to shore and near weed beds.

# 23 WHITE BASS

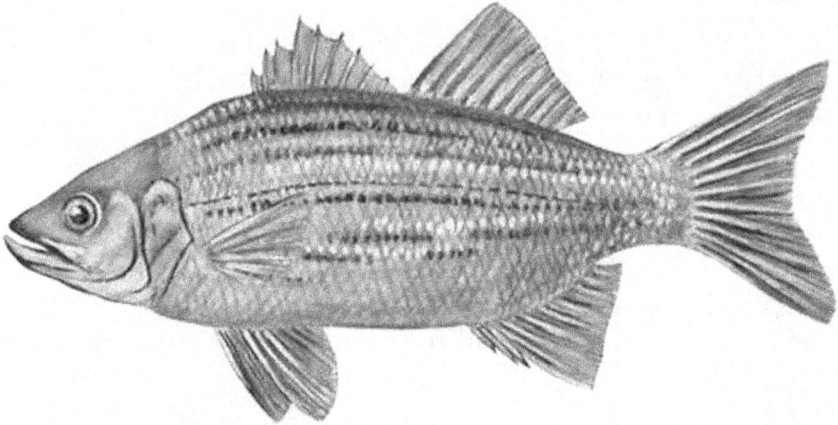

The white bass belongs to the family Moronidae. It is not in the same family as the smallmouth bass and the largemouth bass. Because of this the smallmouth and largemouth are often called black bass. The smallmouth and largemouth belong in the family Centrarchidae along with rock bass, sunfish, and crappies. The scientific name of the white bass is *Roccus chrysops* Rafinesque.

The white bass has a deep body. The back is silvery green. The sides are silvery white and it is golden below. The eye has a golden iris. There are two dorsal fins on the arched back. The first spiny dorsal fin is distinctly separated from the second soft dorsal fin. (In the Centrarchidae the dorsal fins are not separated.)

White bass spawn in late May or early June when the water temperature is between 14° C and 24° C. The spawning grounds are near shore in waters three to six feet deep. The males are smaller than the females and arrive at the spawning grounds first. Eggs and sperm are scattered simultaneously near the surface or in mid-water. The fertilized eggs sink and adhere to the rocks on the bottom.

The favourite food of the white bass are fish. They eat emerald shiners, perch, bluegill, bullhead, and game fish. They also eat aquatic insects, crayfish, and plankton.

## WHERE TO FISH FOR WHITE BASS

White bass travel in large schools near the surface of open water in June, July, and August. They have been taken on quiet shores and on the open lake. Schools can be readily seen by a characteristic commotion. When feeding near the surface, these fish will take almost any type of bait. They also occur near the bottom in small schools.

# 24 SHEEPSHEAD

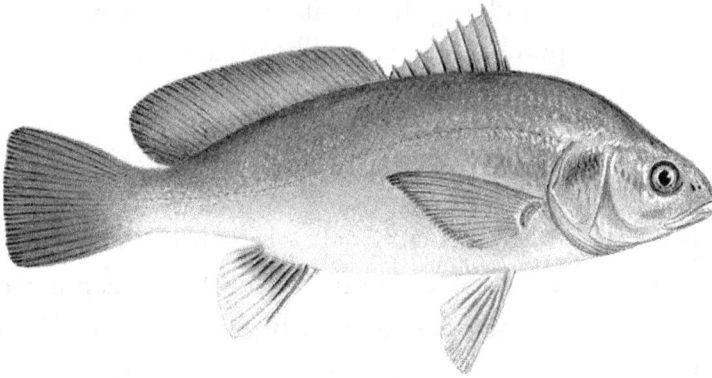

The sheepshead also known as fresh water drum, is the only fresh water member of a large ocean family including such well-known sports fish as the channel bass, weakfish, and kingfish. Its other common names such as croaker, grunter, and thunderpumper refer to grunting noises that the fish makes with its swim bladder. The scientific name is *Aplodinosus grunniens* Rafinesque.

The sheepshead is frequently mistaken for a bass. In fact, the smallmouth bass divisions of large fishing contests have been won by sheepshead in the past. Although the sheepshead has the general shape of a bass and a similar double dorsal fin, they can easily be separated by the silvery sides of the sheepshead and its rounded tail.

Freshwater drum eat fish, molluscs, and crayfish. Sheephead have been reported reaching 50 to 60 pounds but in Lake Nipissing, the maximum is 30 pounds. Fish taken by anglers average 5 pounds but 10 pounders are not uncommon.

The inner ears of sheepshead contain bony stones called otoliths. These are considered to be lucky by some fishermen and can be buffed into attractive jewellery.

Sheepsheads are in water less than 33 feet deep. They spawn in June through July when the water temperature reaches 18° C. Females randomly release their eggs into the water column in the open lake. The eggs are then fertilized by the males. The eggs float to the surface where they hatch in two to four days.

## WHERE TO FISH FOR SHEEPSHEAD

Sheepshead can be found in shallow water areas throughout the lake. Often in the same areas as common suckers. Specific areas where they are known to be abundant on occasions include the Dokis Point area, the north shore of Sandy Island, and Callander Bay.

# 25 BURBOT

The burbot is seldom referred to by anglers as burbot, the more common names used are ling, freshwater cod, maria, lawyer and eelpout, and the French call it Lotte. It's scientific name is *Lota lota* Linnaeus.

The ling is an elongated fish. The front half of the body is more or less rounded while the tail portion is laterally compressed. This fish is distinguished from all other fresh water fishes by the single small, but well developed barbel on the chin. The dorsal fin is approximately one half of the total length of the fish. The fish ranges in colour from light brown to almost black. Lake Nipissing ling have an average weight of from 3 to 5 pounds.

The ling is a relative of the marine cod and like the Atlantic codfish, the ling liver provides oil similar in all respects to cod liver oil.

The burbots spawn in the winter from January to March. They spawn on the sandy bottoms and gravelly shoals.

Burbot eat gammarids, crayfish and fish. They sometimes kill fish their own size.

## WHERE TO FISH FOR BURBOT

During the summer the burbot seeks the deep, cool water of the French River, but during other seasons of the year, it may be found at all depths. Anglers take them in fairly large numbers when ice fishing for other species and when pre-baiting for whitefish.

There are no restrictions on angling for burbot. They bite readily when live minnows are used as bait. During the spring and fall, successful burbot angling can be had in shallow areas near the mouths of tributaries to the lake in the early morning or evening. During the summer, angling for burbot is at a low ebb, although they can be taken by deep hook and line fishing in the French River area.

It is during the winter that burbot angling becomes most appealing. Fishing is done in 15 to 75 feet of water through holes cut in the ice.

Burbot fishing may be conducted at night. Since winter nights are cold, the wise fisherman provides himself with a windproof house placed over a hole.

A small pailful of salted minnows should be scattered over the bottom where the fisherman places his house. The baited hook is allowed to rest on the bottom. A bobber or tip-up is used while angling from fishing huts, but just a line, sinker, and baited hook may be used.

# 26 GOLDEN SHINER

The scientific name of golden shiner is Notemigonus crysolucas. It belongs to the family Cyprinidae, which includes true minnows and carp. The body is laterally compressed. Its back is dark green or olive. The bottom is white and the sides are golden. In smaller individuals the sides are silvery. The golden shiner is usually at a length of 3 to 4.9 inches.

During the spawning period, females lay about 200,000 sticky eggs in vegetation. Some golden shiners deposit their eggs into the occupied nests of sunfish and largemouth bass. Thus their eggs and young are protected by the male of the sunfish or largemouth bass who is guarding that particular nest. The young sunfish and largemouth bass get along very well with the golden shiner fry.

Golden shiners are omnivorous. They eat insects, plants and algae. They feed at the surface, in the mid water, and at the bottom. Golden shiners live in large schools and roam widely.

## FISHING

Golden shiners are often used as bait fish.

# 27 NORTHERN COMMON SHINER

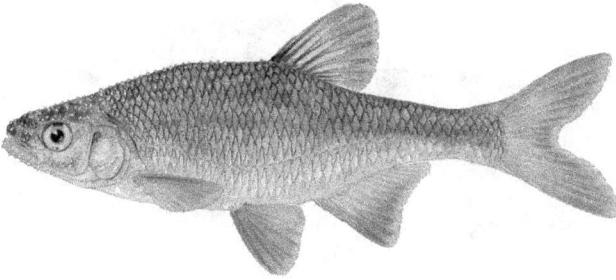

The scientific name of the northern common shiner is Notropis cornutus. It is a silvery colour with an olive back and dark dorsal stripes. The colour is also sometimes bronze. Breeding males have a pinkish tint over their body and have tubercles or bumps on their head. Compared to other small minnows, the head, eyes, and mouth are large.

The common shiner spawns in May and June when the water temperature is 16° C to 26° C. They build nests in the shallows of the lake. Sometimes, they lay their eggs in the nests of chub. The male guards the nest.

The northern common shiner eat aquatic and terrestrial insects, vegetation, and small fish. They are usually found measuring 4 to 6 inches. Sometimes, they reach a length of 8 inches.

# 28 FINE SCALED DACE

The scientific name is *Chrosomus neogaeus* Cope. It gets its name from the fine scales running along its body. The body is bronze and black. It has dark bands running parallel to its body. The head is large and blunt.

Spawning occurs in April when the temperature reaches 15° C. The female lays her eggs on the bottom underneath waterlogged timber and brush. The eggs sink to the bottom where the male fertilizes them. The eggs are left unattended by the parents.

The fine scaled dace eat plankton, algae, crustaceans, water beetles, and other insects. They reach a size from 2.4 to 2.8 inches.

## FISHING AND FINE SCALED DACE

Fine scaled dace are sold as bait fish in bait shops. They are also sold as pets for home aquariums.

# 29 STRAW-COLOURED MINNOW

The straw-coloured minnow is also called the sand shiner. Its scientific name is *Notropis stramineus* Cope. It has a compressed slender body with a silvery head, and sides with a dark mid dorsal strip extending to the anal fin. It also has a thin lateral strip on its side.

The peak spawning period occurs in July and August when the water temperature is 27° C to 37° C. Eggs are laid in shallow water over sandy substrate.

The straw-coloured minnow feed in large schools in shallow water. They eat bottom ooze, aquatic and terrestrial insects, and plant matter. They have a length of 1.7 to 3.2 inches.

# 30 SPOT-TAILED MINNOW

The spot-tailed minnow is also called the spot-tailed shiner. The scientific name is *Notropis hudsonius* Clinton. It has a slightly compressed, elongated body. It has a compressed subterminal mouth. There is a distinct black spot at the base of the caudal fin. The dorsal side of this fish is silvery to pale green or olive. The lower edge of the caudal fin may be white in colour. All the other fins lack pigment. There is a complete lateral line running horizontally along its sides.

The spawning season takes place in June and July. They spawn near the shore on sandy bottoms.

The spot-tail minnow eats water fleas, plant material, algae, vascular plants, caddisflies, mayflies, remains of macro invertebrates, and nematodes. It obtains much of its food by scavenging the lake bottom, and it does not prey on other fish species. The average size of spot tail shiners is two to three inches. They may reach a size of six inches.

# 31 LAKE SHINER

The lake shiner is also called the emerald shiner. The scientific name is *Notropis atherinoides* Rafinesque. The lake shiner is bright iridescent silvery green. The back and upper sides are emerald green to straw-coloured. The body is slender, laterally compressed, and the dorsal fin is transparent. The snout is short and blunt.

Lake shiners have spawned anytime from mid May to mid August when the water temperature is 20.1° C to 23.2° C.

The lake shiner eats zooplankton, protozoans, and diatoms. At dusk the emerald shiners follow the plankton food source to the surface. At the surface they also eat aquatic and terrestrial insects. When dawn comes, the shiners move back down to the bottom. It can grow to 3.5 inches in length.

## FISHING

Emerald shiners are used as bait fish. Some people use them as aquarium fish because of their glistening silvery appearance.

# 32 BLUNTNOSE MINNOW

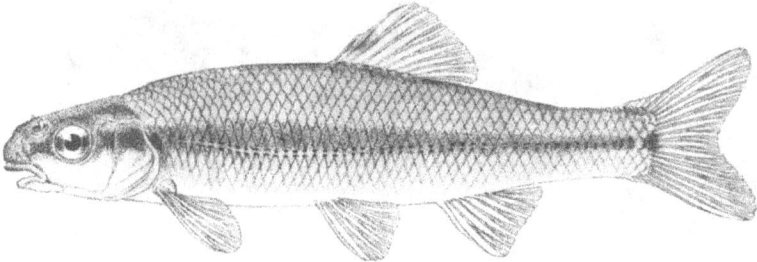

The scientific name of the bluntnose minnow is *Pimephales notatus* Rafinesque. It has a rounded head with a terminal mouth. The snout hangs a little bit over the mouth giving the blunt nose appearance. The upper body is pale olive and the lower body is silvery. There are dark pigmented spots on the first two or three dorsal rays. A darkish lateral line runs from its head ending with a dark spot at the tail.

Spawning takes place from early spring to mid summer. Their eggs are attached under stones in depressions which they have dug. During the mating season the males heads become dark and their bodies bluish.

The bluntnose minnow eats aquatic insects, insect larvae, algae, and small crustaceans. They average a length of 2.6 inches and may reach a length of 4.3 inches. They prefer clear shallow water with a sandy bottom. The bluntnose minnows are found in large schools and also often found alone.

## FISHING

The bluntnose minnow is a popular bait fish.

# 33 LAKE CHUB

The scientific name of lake chub is *Coueiuss plumbeus* Agassis. The body is fusiform and is elongated. The upper body is olive brown or dark brown. The sides are leaden silver. The blunt snout projects slightly beyond the upper lip. There is a small barbel on each corner of the mouth. The mouth is small and the tail is forked. This fish has no teeth.

Lake chubs spawn in the early summer. They migrate streams where they lay their eggs during either the day or the night. The eggs are released over gravel or rocks. There is no parental care.

The lake chub eats algae, zooplankton, aquatic insect larvae, and insects. The largest individuals also eat small fish. It is usually 4 to 7 inches long. The largest individuals may reach a length of 9 inches.

## FISHING

The lake chub is often used as bait fish.

# 34 FATHEAD MINNOW

*By Duane Raver/ U. S. Fish and Wildlife Service, Public Domain.*

The scientific name of the fathead minnow is *Pimephales promalas* Rafinesque. The colour is a dull olive grey. It has a dark stripe running along the back and sides. The underside is lighter to white. There is a dark blotch midway on the dorsal fin.

They begin to spawn when the water temperature reaches 18° C. Then they spawn several times, continuing until the water temperature falls below 18° C. The female lays her eggs in nests and the male guards the nests. They prefer to lay their eggs in nests already containing eggs; the more the better. The male will chase the inhabiting male from the nest and take over the guarding of the nest. Thus several deposits of eggs may reside in one nest. A short time after spawning the adults die.

The fathead minnow is omnivorous. It filters the bottom muck for food material (bottom detritus). They also eat algae, zooplankton, insects, crustaceans, and other aquatic invertebrates.

## FISHING

Fathead minnows are very popular as bait fish.

# 35 REDBELLY DACE

The redbelly dace is a member of the family Cyprinidae. The scientific name of redbelly dace is *Chrosomus eos* Cope. This fish grows to only a little bit over two inches long. The back is iridescent silver. There are two dusky longitudinal stripes on its sides. The lower sides of the body are white, yellow, or silver. This part of the body becomes brilliant red on the males during breeding season.

Redbally dace spawn in the spring around May. The eggs are laid in filamentous algae.

The redbelly dace eat mainly filamentous algae, diatoms, zooplankton, and insect larvae.

# 36 MUD MINNOW

The scientific name of the mud minnow is *Umbra limi* Kirtland. It belongs to the family Umbridae.

It is brownish on top with with mottled sides and a pale belly. It has a modified gas bladder which enables it to breathe air.

The mud minnow spawns in shallow water in mid April when the water is 13° C.

Mud minnows travel in schools and eat zooplanktons, macro invertebrates, gastropods, and chironomids. They reach lengths of two to four inches. When threatened, they bury themselves in the mud tail first.

## FISHING

Mud minnows are used as bait fish.

# 37 TROUT PERCH

The scientific name of trout perch is *Percopsis omiscomaycus* Walbaum. It belongs to the family Percopsidae. It is silvery or nearly transparent with rows of dark spots along its sides. Its fins are transparent and it has an adipose fin like a trout. It has a long head, a long snout, and a small mouth.

The trout perch spawn from May through August. When the water temperature is between 20° C and 23° C they spawn on sand bars and on rocks. The female is surrounded by three or four males who fertilize the eggs as they are released by the female. The young and the eggs receive parental care.

The trout perch travel from deep water during the day to shallow water during the night when they do their feeding. They eat zooplanktons, insect larvae, and crustaceans. The larger adults also eat small fish like Johnny darter. They are usually about 3.5 inches in length. Some individuals reach a length of 7.9 inches.

## FISHING

Trout perch are occasionally used as bait.

# 38 NINE SPINED STICKLEBACK

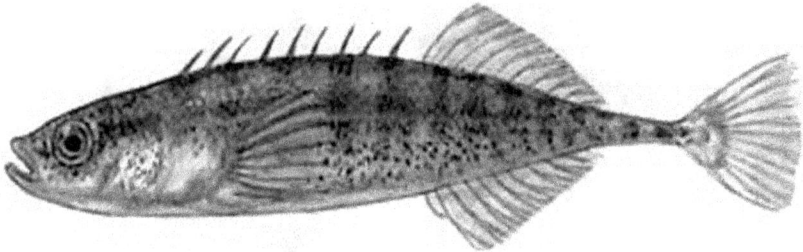

The nine spined stickleback belongs to the family Gasterosteidae. Its scientific name is *Pungitius pungitius* Linnaeus.

The body of the nine spined stickleback tapers to a very narrow caudal peduncle and the caudal (tail) fin is shaped like a fan. The number of spines in front of the dorsal fin varies from seven to twelve. Nine is the number most common. Some people call it the ten spined stickleback. The colour is greyish to olive brown. The sides are silvery with dark blotches or bars of dark colour. The mouth points upwards.

The female lays her eggs in a nest built by the male. The nest is suspended on a piece of water weed about an inch above the bottom. After the eggs are laid, the female leaves. The male guards the nest and the young fry when they emerge. When the young have their spines the male drives them away to look after themselves.

The nine spined stickleback eats the eggs and young of other fish. It reaches a size of 2 to 3 inches.

# 39 LOG PERCH

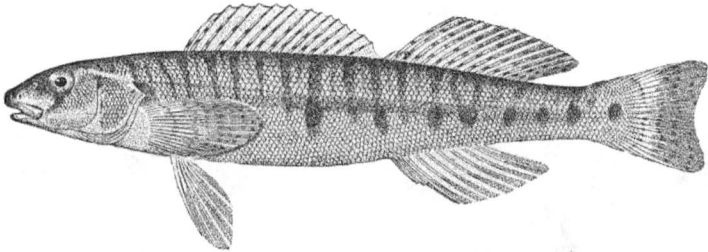

The log perch is a member of the family Percidae. Its scientific name is *Percina caprodes* Rafinesque. It has dark barring along its sides. The mouth is subterminal.

The log perch spawns numerous times during the spring and the summer. They lay adhesive eggs which stick between rocks and other substrates on shallow rocky shoals. The hatched embryos drift to lentic areas where the fry feed on plankton

It hunts by flipping over stones with its snout. Its food is mainly chironomids. It also eats benthic invertebrates. It reaches a maximum size of 7.1 inches.

# 40 JOHNNY DARTER

Johnny darter belongs to the family Percidae. It is small and slender. It is brown to yellow with paler sides and a whitish belly. It has brown or black markings on its sides in the shapes of X or W. The opercles (bony areas covering the gills) have scales.

Johnny darters spawn in the spring. The male prepares a nest under rocks. The female lays 30 to 100 eggs in the nest. Several females often lay their eggs in one nest. The male then guards the nest until the eggs hatch.

Johnny darter feeds on chironomid (midge fly larvae) and other aquatic insect larvae. They grow to a length of 2.8 inches.

# 41 IOWA DARTER

The Iowa darter belongs to the family Percidae. Its scientific name is *Etheostoma exile* Girard. It has a thin small body with a small snout and mouth. It has two dorsal fins. The front dorsal is spiny rayed. The other has soft rays. The pectoral fins are located behind the gills and are close to each other. The caudal (tail) fin is kind of squarish and it has two anal fins. Males and females have different colour patterns. During breeding season the males are olivaceous dorsally with darker spots along their back. Their sides are red with blue rectangular blotches with a dark wedge shape below the eyes. The bottom half of the dorsal fin has blue spots between the spines. Above the spots is a succession of three bands, orange on the bottom, clear in the middle, and blue on the outside. Females are olive brown with darker spots across the back. The sides are mottled and fade to a silver white on their belly.

Iowa darters lack swim bladders so they swim along the bottom over sandy or organic bottoms. They are found in shallow water. The Iowa darter eats copepods, mayfly larvae and midges. They make short dashes of astonishing speeds faster than a human eye can follow. They are not caught by predators because of their astonishing speed. They reach a size of two inches.

Iowa darters spawn in shallow water when the temperature is 13° C to 16° C. In the spring, the males arrive at the spawning sites first and set up territories. When a female enters a male's territory, he courts her by swimming around her. The female situates herself near algae or rooted vegetation. The male mounts her, positioning himself so that his pelvic fins are in front of her dorsal fin. During each spawning act, three to seven eggs are deposited. The female mates with several males. After spawning the females head for deeper water. The males stay and guard their territories and in this way protect the eggs.

# 42 EASTERN SLIMY SCULPIN

The eastern slimy sculpin belongs to the family Cottidae. Its scientific name is *Cottus cognatus* Richardson. Its mouth and snout are very wide and terminal. The first dorsal fin is narrow with 7 to nine soft spines. The second dorsal fin has 16 to 18 fin rays. The sides, back, and head are dark brown olive with mottled with dark irregular blotches. It has a pair of free independent pelvic fins.

The slimy sculpin has no swim bladder so it can not swim in mid water. It has to move along the bottom. When it lies motionless, it is camouflaged so well into its surroundings that it is almost impossible to see it. When the fish is moving it does so in rapid dart like motions so that it looks like it is hopping.

The preferred water temperature is 9° C to 14° C. They spawn in late April and May. During the mating season, the first dorsal fin of the male becomes orange which attracts the females. The males find nesting sites under stones or tree roots. The male attracts a female to the nest and eggs are laid and fertilized. The male then chases the female away. After the female is gone, the male attracts another female to the nest and mating occurs again. The males protect the nest and protects the young after they have hatched.

The sculpin eats mayflies, caddis flies, dragonflies, and stone flies. Sometimes it also eats fish eggs and small fish. They reach a size of 2.5 to 3.6 inches.

# 43 NORTHERN MOTTLED SCULPIN

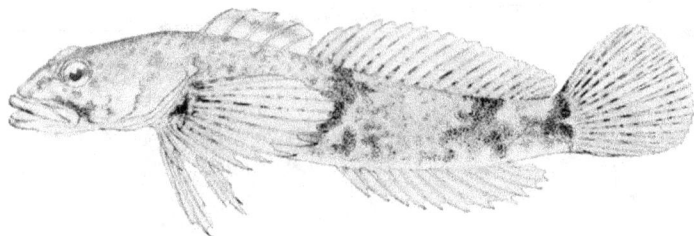

The northern mottled sculpin belongs to the family Cottidae. Its scientific name is *Cottus bairdii* Girard.

Its colour is a combination of spots, bars and speckles randomly distributed. The large pectoral fins are banded.

Mottled sculpins breed during April and May. The male fashions a nest under a flat bottomed rock or water logged wood. The female enters the nest, turns upside down, and lays her eggs on the ceiling to which they adhere. The clutch size varies between 8 eggs and 148 eggs. Several females lay eggs in a nest.

The male chases the female away after the eggs are laid. Sometimes, he eats her if she is small. The male guards the nest and the hatchlings until the yolk sacks have been absorbed.

Sculpin are bottom dwellers by necessity because they have no air bladder to make them bouyant. They eat aquatic insects and their larvae. The male will eat smaller females. If a young hatchling becomes infected with a fungus or a virus, the male will eat it. Female mottled sculpin live in clean water with rocky substrates. The males are found in algae beds.

## 44 SILVER LAMPREY

The silver lamprey belongs to the family Petromyzontidae. Its scientific name is *Ichyomyzon unicuspis* Hubbs & Trautman. It is an eel like fish with a cartilagenous skeleton. It is a dull brown or tan colour. The dorsal fin is continuous, often notched. The seven gill openings are arranged in a straight line behind the eye. It does not have paired fins. The mouth is a jawless sucking disc. The mouth has unicuspid teeth arranged in circular rows.

Adult silver lamprey move upstream to spawn in May and June, when the water temperature is 10° C. With their mouths they build nests in the stream bed. When the nest is complete, the female attaches herself to a rock. The male attaches himself to the female's head and their bodies intertwine. After the eggs and sperm are released the pair separate. The eggs are deposited in the nest and the adults die. The larvae are called ammocetes. They are blind and toothless.

The ammocetes drift down stream and burrow into sand or mud. The ammocetes are filter feeders and eat detritus and algae. They stay in the mud for 4 or 7 years. When they reach a size of 4 or 5 inches in length they undergo metamorphosis and become young adults. They then migrate downstream into the lake to search for hosts. They attach themselves to a host fish with their sucker mouths and cut through scales and skin with their teeth. They stay on their host for a long period of time gaining nourishment from the blood of the host. Very seldom is a host ever killed from this effect. After two years the silver lamprey returns to the stream to reproduce and die.

# 45 FISHERIES MANAGEMENT

A fisheries research laboratory was established in Frank's Bay in 1929. This was a part of the University of Toronto studies. The actual establishing of the laboratory was carried out by Dr. William John Knox Harkness. The graduate students located there did extensive studies of the fish of Lake Nipissing. The fisheries laboratory was discontinued in the 1930's.

Managing fishes is done by long range forecasting. This involves extensive studies of the fish and their habitat. Estimates of relative numbers are used. Deriving these estimates may be divided into two groups. One is trends in total catch and catch per unit effort. The second is trends in catch and age class composition. The first group gives a fairly clear indication of trends in numbers, but a more accurate result is usually provided by counts of year classes in catches. Satisfactory forecasts are obtained for some species on the basis of sizes of year class strength together with an analysis of the growth and age class composition. This forecast is then used to develop a management plan.

The Lake Nipissing Fisheries Assessment Unit was established in 1970 to study the population dynamics of the Lake Nipissing sport species. The information was then used to make management decisions. The study and management decisions are discussed in my book "Trying To Work For The M. N. R." The Lake Nipissing Fisheries Assessmant Unit was discontinued in 1996 for political reasons.

Managing fresh water fishes is made difficult because many people seem to believe that they know more than the fisheries biologists. When management actions are proposed there are people who will say, "Do not limit my fishing. Limit the fishing of those people over there."

# 46 FISH STOCKING

For over 100 years the artificial propagation of fish in hatcheries in North America was believed to be the chief method of maintaining stocks of fish in lakes and streams. Indeed it became the belief of the general public. However, it has been found, as a result of research and experience, that artificial propagation does not pay except for the following conditions:

1. Where conditions are favourable for growth but not for reproduction.

2. To reintroduce a species in waters from which it has been eliminated due to winter kill or by release of a lethal pollutant.

3. To introduce exotic species where conditions have made the waters no longer tenable by native species.

4. Where it is considered necessary to provide fishing beyond the carrying capacity of a particular body of water. The least expensive way to provide fishing under such circumstances is to plant legal-sized fish immediately before they are caught.

In the 1980's there were heavy cutbacks in the M.N.R. Many people still believed that the chief method of maintaining stocks of fish in lakes was by stocking. Some of these people were demanding that this be done in Lake Nipissing. The Minister of Natural Resources, Mike Harris, had made an election promise that Lake Nipissing would have a walleye hatchery.

To build a hatchery would cost several million dollars. It would also be much more expensive to run than the existing hatcheries. This is because the existing hatcheries were trout hatcheries. Trout are cold water fish. A walleye hatchery would need heated water which would increase the cost of running it enormously.

The result was that a "jar hatchery" was developed. Thus when I had a crew tagging spawners at Wasi Falls, a crew of a half dozen men or more would show up to take spawn. Eggs were taken from female spawners into a pan. Milt from male spawners were mixed with the eggs. The fertilized eggs were put into big jars which were in a shed. Walleye eggs are sticky so that they adhere to the bottom substrate and not be swept away by the stream current. To keep the eggs from sticking to each other and forming one big clump, the water in the jars was constantly circulated.

Ponds were constructed in which the young walleye were raised to fry size. But these walleye were stunted. If the food supply of young walleye (e.g., young of year yellow perch) outgrow the young of year walleye, the walleye will have no food and therefore starve to death. The young of year walleye released from the rearing pond was the same size as the young of year yellow perch which is their main food supply.

In my opinion, the jar hatcheries were the wrong answer to stocking walleye. The 4 conditions, mentioned above, did not exist for Lake Nipissing. The stocking of fishes in Lake Nipissing is, at this point, not necessary. However, if in the future the need for stocking arises then it would be in the best interests of the lake and the anglers to spend the money to build a proper hatchery.

CARSTEN R. JORGENSEN

# 47 GLOSSARY

**Adipose Fin** - a soft, fleshy fin found on the back behind the dorsal fin

**Ammocetes** — the larval stage of a lamprey

**Anal Fin** — fin pertaining to, or near the anus

**Barbels** - a slender, whiskerlike sensory organ near the mouth

**Benthic** - the ecological region at the lowest level of a body of water, including the sediment surface and some sub-surface layers

**Chironomid** - midge fly

**Cladocerans** - small crustaceans often found in most freshwater habitats; commonly called water fleas

**Copepods** - tiny marine or freshwater crustaceans with large antenae and short cylindrical bodies that are divided into a number of segments

**Caudal** - at or near the tail or the posterior end of the body

**Caudal peduncle** - the narrow part of the body to which the tail attaches.

**Detritus** — waste or debris; matter produced by the decay or disintegration of an organic substance.

**Diatoms** - unicellular or colonial green algae

**Dorsal Fin** - fin situated on or toward the upper side of the body, equivalent to the back, or posterior, in humans

**Gammarids** - crustaceans of the order Amphipod. Amphipods resemble, and are often mistaken for, tiny shrimp

**Gastropods** – snails and slugs

**Gibbous** - bulging, convex, hump, hunchback

**Hellgrammites** - the aquatic larvae of the Dobsonfly

**Lentic** - situated in still, fresh water

**Opercles** - membrane bones located behind the cheeks and covering the gills

**Otoliths** - a calcium carbonate structure in the inner ear.. Some anglers buff these into attractive jewellery

**Pectoral Fin**- fin pertaining to the chest or breast; thorax.

**Pharynx** - part of the throat that is behind the mouth and nasal cavity; the tubes going down to the stomach and the lungs

**Protozoans** - single celled organisms

**Subterminal** – the mouth is on the underside of the head

**Tubercles** - a round nodule, or warty outgrowth

**Unicuspid** - having one cusp or point

**Ventral** - the underside of an animal or plant; abdominal; belly

# 48 REFERENCES

Dymond, J.R. 1964. Fish and Wildlife. A Memorial to W.J.K. Harkness. Longmans Canada Limited, Toronto. 206 pp.

Jorgensen, C.R. 2016. Trying To Work For The M.N.R. 185 pp.

MacKay, H.H. 1963. Fishes Of Ontario. The Bryant Press Limited, Toronto. 300 pp.

CARSTEN R. JORGENSEN

# ABOUT THE AUTHOR

Carsten Jorgensen dedicated thirty years in studying and managing fisheries for the Ontario Ministry of Natural Resources.

Upon graduation from Queen's University in Kingston, Ontario in 1966, he accepted a biologist position on Lake Temagami with the Ontario Department of Lands and Forests.

In 1968 he also started work on Lake Nipissing. In 1970 Mr. Jorgensen was working full time as the Lake Nipissing Fisheries Assessment Unit Biologist.

In 1970 he married Brenda Black, daughter of Ontario Conservation Officer, Gordon Black.

In 1996 he retired and now enjoys spending his time playing chess, playing darts, doing Tai Chi, and writing books.

CARSTEN R. JORGENSEN

## OTHER TITLES BY CARSTEN R. JORGENSEN

If you enjoyed this book by Carsten R. Jorgensen, you may also enjoy these other books that he has written:

**The Saga Kings** -
ISBN-13: 978-0994933805

**Trying To Work For The M.N.R.** -
ISBN-13: 978-0-9949338-1-2

**My World War Two Adventures In Denmark** -
ISBN-13: 978-0-9949338-2-9

**One School, Two School, Old School, New School** -
ISBN-13: 978-0-9949338-3-6

Or check out his author profile on Good Reads for any new and upcoming books he may be working on:

www.goodreads.com/author/show/14680643.Carsten_R_Jorgensen